People

YEARBOOK
2013!

CONTENTS

14

6

8

90

34

President Barack Obama and his family
(from left, wife Michelle and daughters Sasha
and Malia) celebrate after a long campaign.

What a year! A tough election; a nasty hurricane; celebrity splits galore (Tom and Katie, Ashton and Demi); sports triumph (Olympian Gabby Douglas) and disappointment (Lance Armstrong); a humongous ring (for newly engaged Jennifer Aniston); a hit ("Call Me Maybe"); and a Honey Boo Boo

FIRST FAMILY, TAKE TWO

After the most expensive election in U.S. history—$6 billion, by some estimates—the country wound up . . . almost exactly where it was before: Barack Obama, 51, is President; Democrats control the Senate (and picked up two seats); and Republicans held the House. Super pac money unleashed by the Supreme Court's Citizens United decision failed to turn the electoral tide, as many had predicted (the largest donor on record, Las Vegas businessman Sheldon Adelson, gave more than $53 million to Republican nominee Mitt Romney and other conservative candidates but saw only one of his favorites win).

The election's other winner: statistician/blogger Nate Silver, who, as breathless TV pundits called the presidential race a nail-biting dead heat, calmly and repeatedly said the electoral vote was a virtual lock for Obama. In the end, Silver called all 50 states correctly.

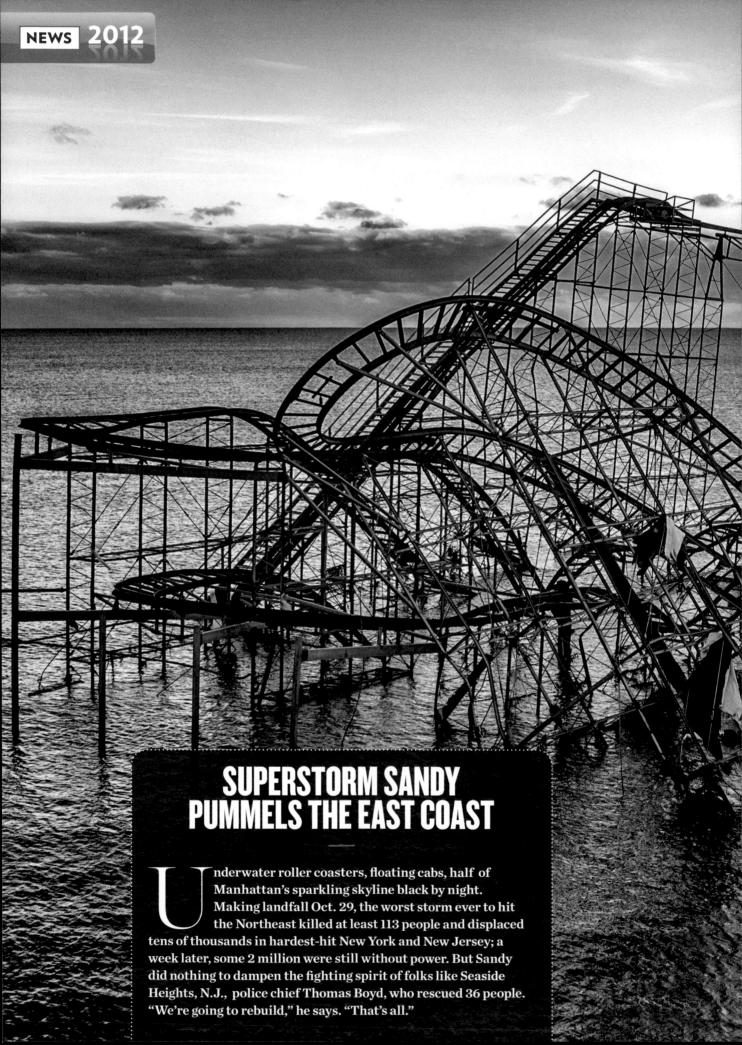

SUPERSTORM SANDY PUMMELS THE EAST COAST

Underwater roller coasters, floating cabs, half of Manhattan's sparkling skyline black by night. Making landfall Oct. 29, the worst storm ever to hit the Northeast killed at least 113 people and displaced tens of thousands in hardest-hit New York and New Jersey; a week later, some 2 million were still without power. But Sandy did nothing to dampen the fighting spirit of folks like Seaside Heights, N.J., police chief Thomas Boyd, who rescued 36 people. "We're going to rebuild," he says. "That's all."

WATER EVERYWHERE Sandy cut a 900-mile-wide swath and caused an estimated $50 billion in damage. Left: Waves destroyed a Seaside Heights, N.J., pier, toppling a roller coaster into the Atlantic. Top to bottom: wrecked boats in Monmouth Beach, N.J.; police rescue a Staten Island child; water-logged cabs in Hoboken, N.J.; a car left on a wall in Staten Island.

A PRINCESS GOES TO WORK

It may be one of the longest royal honeymoons on record: More than a year after a spectacular and romantic wedding to Prince William, his wife, Kate, hadn't put a foot wrong—with the public, the press or, perhaps most important, her grandmother-in-law, the Queen of England. "She has a lot invested in this couple," says Robert Lacey, author of *The Queen: A Life in Brief.* "She thinks Kate's her girl."

Except for one notable hiccup—more about that in a minute—the Queen probably could not have been happier. Not since Di had anyone pumped such life into the fusty, even sclerotic, institution of British Royalty. A most uncommon commoner, Kate, in year one, came across as demure, stylish, hardworking and without pretense. In Angelsey, where William and Kate live while he serves in the Royal Air Force, they stop by the local pub and Kate shops at the Tesco market. "We wave, and she waves back," says a resident. "It's like she's one of us." Adds another local: "They don't get hassled here."

On the job, she's similarly approachable. While William was stationed in the Falklands for six weeks last winter, Kate, for the first time, made a string of public appearances on her own and got great reviews. During a Valentine's Day visit to an oncology unit at Alder Hey Children's Hospital in Liverpool, she chatted easily with kids about the hometown soccer team and her new cocker spaniel puppy, Lupo. "It's a special gift to get that instant rapport with children," said Lisa Casey, whose son Elliot talked with the Duchess. "She'll be good at her job." Later, at an addiction treatment center, Kate sat in the audience as Rachel Lyons, 36 and sober

A GOOD SPORT IN A GRASS SKIRT: Kate took dress and dance advice during a trip to the Solomon Islands. Above: Prince William and Kate on parade on Guadalcanal Island.

Still hung up on you: William and Kate, up a tree in Malaysia in September.

public." That she's able to stay that way may be testimony to William and Kate's concerted effort to maintain a private life. "They've got various compartments," says a well-placed insider. "There's the royal duties, the royal family, the Middleton family and their close team of friends. Their friends keep them normal."

William and Kate likely turned to those friends during the only blemish in an otherwise stellar year: On Sept. 14, a French magazine, *Closer*, published topless pictures of Kate, taken with a long lens from half a mile away, while the couple was vacationing in southern France. William and Kate, on a tour of the South Pacific at the time, were outraged. *Closer* "invaded their privacy in . . . a grotesque and totally unjustifiable manner," said the Palace in a statement. "This incident is reminiscent of the worst excesses of the press and paparazzi during the life of Diana, Princess of Wales, and all the more upsetting to the duke and duchess for being so." Said a hometown friend of Kate's: "I would imagine she is absolutely gutted."

Nonetheless, she handled it in a way that, no doubt, the Queen would approve: She put a smile on her face and got back to work. "People love them because we see them as ordinary people with fairy dust," says Harris. "And this is what a real girl does. When things go wrong, you put on a brave face. She's tougher than people give her credit for."

for a year, described how alcoholism had strained her relationship with her children. Later, Kate met with her privately. "She said it was really well done for me to get up and speak like that," recalled Lyons. "It felt wonderful that our future Queen was sitting in front of me, listening."

Whatever the event, making a personal

connection appears to be her goal. "She seems to have fallen into it easily," says Colleen Harris, former public relations director for Princes Charles, William and Harry. "I think that's because William has given her lots of support and the space to do it gradually." Adds a Palace source: "She is genuine, both in private and in

KATE ON THE JOB

MEET THE PRESS (clockwise from top): Kate and her father-in-law, Prince Charles, made artwork and ironed it onto silk at a London gallery in March; with the Queen (who never made an official appearance with Princess Diana or Fergie during their first year of marriage to her sons); visiting a child and planting a tree at East Anglia Children's Hospices; and joining inner-city kids at the Expanding Horizons Primary School camp in Kent.

RADIANT IN RED

The remarkably photogenic Princess has won raves for her fashion sense, a lively mix of style and fun. And even, recently, a touch of sexy: In May, when she stepped from a navy blue Jaguar while wearing a sleek emerald gown and 4-inch Jimmy Choos, "there was an audible, 'Wow'," says royal photographer Mark Stewart.

PRINCELY PDA

In public, William and Kate (left, strolling on a Welsh beach and, above, at the Olympic Velodrome in August) seem both at ease and in love—a combination that's not unusual for newlyweds, but is rare, if not unique, in recent Windsor history.

STARBURST: Houston's mentor, producer Clive Davis, promoted the 19-year-old with language that would make a carnival barker blush, saying, "There was Lena Horne. There is Dionne Warwick. But if the mantle is to pass to somebody . . . who's elegant, who's sensuous . . . who's got an incredible range of talent . . . it will be Whitney Houston." He was right.

WHITNEY HOUSTON

That voice. That smile. That light-up-your-life energy. Whitney Houston would have been a star in any age, but as the total made-for-MTV package in a world newly gone crazy for music videos, she probably went further, faster than any pop star in history. Her record seven No. 1 hits in a row—beginning in 1985 with "Saving All My Love for You" and including "Didn't We Almost Have It All" and "I Will Always Love You" —beat the Beatles; her first album, *Whitney Houston*, became, at the time, the bestselling debut by a female. In her '80s glory, a critic wrote, everyone wanted to "adopt her, escort her or be her."

But even then, a Houston relative said after her death, "she was never what you all thought she was. She could swear like a sailor, and they were always worried she was going to drop the F-word in public and it would make people not like her." Sadly, the world eventually saw that side of Houston too, during her wild 15-year marriage to Bobby Brown and her long battle with drug addiction. On Feb. 11, hours before the Grammys telecast, Houston drowned in her bathtub at the Beverly Hills Hilton. A coroner's report later showed evidence of cocaine use and 12 different medications in her blood.

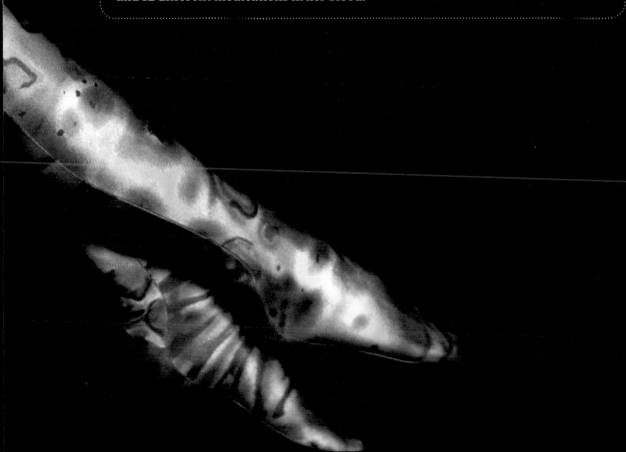

STEALTH SPLIT, STUNNED HUSBAND

It was June 28, and Tom Cruise was astride a motorcycle on the Iceland set of *Oblivion* when he received an unexpected call from his wife, Katie Holmes. "He was about to do a stunt, and he got off his motorcycle to take the call," says a source. What happened next stunned him: Holmes told Cruise, as the film's crew looked on, that she was filing for divorce. Says the source: "He's been in shock since that day."

Understandably; until that moment, Cruise, 50, thought his marriage of five years was just fine. "He was a happy man and thought he had a happy life," says a source. "He keeps asking, 'What's happening?'"

What, indeed? The couple's surprising romance took off like a skyrocket when Cruise, already a megastar, and

Holmes, a teen fave thanks to TV's *Dawson's Creek*, began dating in 2005. His famous couch jumping on *Oprah* accompanied by frequent proclamations of "I LOVE THIS WOMAN!" ramped up the headlines further. Round-the-world photo ops, the 2006 birth of daughter Suri, and the couple's marriage in a 15th-century Italian castle seven months later added to the impression of a fairy tale on steroids. From the outside, it all looked wonderful—and intense.

But while Cruise gushed frequently about the wonders of his marriage—just days before the fateful call, he told PEOPLE "You're blessed to be able to live your dream and have the family that I have, the wife and children that I have"—Holmes, 33, was, publicly, a much more silent partner. Tabloids speculated that she had a difficult time dealing with the key role Tom's devotion to Scientology played in their lives (Cruise has been a Scientologist since the '80s; his three sisters are believers; and the head of the Church, David Miscavige, was best man at Cruise and Holmes's wedding), but Holmes herself kept publicly mum. Friends and family, however, noticed changes. Over time, "Katie went from this beautiful, happy face to this sullen, sad face, and she got sadder and sadder," says a source. "She looked worn down. She was never with any friends—only Suri. I think her parents wanted the old Katie back."

Holmes herself seems to have reached a similar conclusion. Cruise was away almost half of 2011 on film sets; Holmes, staying at their Beverly Hills estate, where his extended family was a constant presence, complained that, "I'm living with your sisters, not you," says a source close to her inner circle. Eventually, says a friend, she realized "she no longer had the life she wanted, in terms of her career, her way of life, everything."

Almost as shocking as the divorce was Holmes's take-charge attitude once her decision was made. "It's clear Tom can be very persuasive and very powerful," says an insider. "But once she decided to go, she was done. She's the daughter of a lawyer; she knew she had to have everything locked down before

she pulled the trigger." Added another source: "It's a real-life *Mission Impossible* when you have people around you who will report back to Tom." Accordingly, Holmes rented a Manhattan apartment, purchased new cell phones and had her father come to New York to fire any associates of hers who might have ties to her husband. Only then did she call Cruise to tell him she was filing.

Although Cruise was stunned, the divorce happened with astonishing speed: Eleven days after filing, both sides signed an agreement giving Holmes custody of Suri and Cruise generous visitation rights (financial issues were taken care of in an ironclad prenup). Cruise settled quickly, said a source, "because he didn't want his family dragged through the mud" in a long public battle. The exes released

An independent woman, Starting over in New York City, Holmes launched a line of clothing during Fashion Week (right), signed on as the face of Bobbi Brown Cosmetics and landed a role in a Broadway comedy, *Dead Accounts*.

a carefully crafted statement saying they are "committed to working together as parents" and—perhaps to defuse speculation that Scientology was a divisive issue—pointedly expressing "respect for each other's commitment to each of our respective beliefs."

As summer turned to fall, Suri was living with her mom in Manhattan and enrolled as a first grader. Cruise, working on a film set in Europe, talked to his daughter every day but "his heart is broken," said his friend, director Christopher McQuarrie. "He misses his little girl and works very hard at parenting."

"They are still very civil to each other and are all about co-parenting," says a Holmes pal of Katie's relationship with Cruise (visiting with Suri at Florida's Disney World).

"She's really such a special girl—strong and funny," Holmes (with Suri in New York), sounding like every mom, told *Glamour*.

SENSELESS HORROR

"We wanted to be the first ones to see it," recalled 14-year-old Prodeo Patria, whose enthusiasm for Batman helped convince his parents to take him to the midnight premiere of *The Dark Knight Rises* at the Century 16 multiplex in Aurora, Colo., July 19. Thirty minutes into the film, a heavily armed man dressed like an action figure in ballistic gear—black helmet, body armor, shin guards and gas mask—stood at the front of the sold-out Theater 9 and opened fire, spraying the terrified crowd with rounds from a shotgun, a .40 caliber semiautomatic pistol and an AR-15 assault rifle. "I kept saying, 'Pray, Mom, pray,'" recalled Patria, who hid with his parents under their seats in the middle of the theater. "I thought I was going to die." The boy and his mother were severely wounded but both survived the savage rampage that left 12 dead and 58 injured. The toll was second only to the 1999 massacre at a high school in nearby Columbine that left 13 victims and their two murderers dead. Among the slain in Aurora were a 6-year-old girl and several victims who were shot and killed as they shielded loved ones from the gunman, James Holmes, 24, a recent dropout from a University of Colorado Ph.D. program who surrendered to police at the scene. "I lost my firstborn," Tom Teves, 52, said of his son Alex, 24, who took a fatal bullet as he used his body to protect his girlfriend. "This," his father said, expressing the thoughts of millions of Americans who have had their fill of tragedy resulting from senseless gun violence, "has got to stop."

ABOVE: "I don't know who he is anymore," a former classmate said of Holmes, a bright but socially awkward neuroscience grad-school dropout whose dazed demeanor and Joker-like dyed hair belied a killer who meticulously prepared for the slaughter, stockpiling weapons, 6,000 rounds of ammunition and even booby-trapping his apartment in an attempt to thwart investigators. Holmes, who appeared in court in September with closely cropped brown hair, faces dozens of counts of murder and attempted murder.

RIGHT (FROM TOP): Mourners at a memorial behind the theater; a ticket stub from the midnight show; Isaac Pacheo at a memorial service for his friend Alex Sullivan, who was killed on his 27th birthday.

CENTURY AURORA
Thu, Jul 19, 2012 11:17 PM
DARK KNIGHT RISES,
Rated: PG-13
Fri 12:05A 07/20/12
Adult Even PREPAID
use:
9
TKT02590342

GABBY DOUGLAS

Your assignment, Mr. Phelps, should you choose to accept it: Go to London. Win medals and lead the U.S. Men's Swimming team to victory. Land many endorsements.

Superswimmer Michael Phelps did, indeed, fulfill what to every mortal before him has been a Mission Impossible: Winning 6 medals (4 gold, 2 silver) at the London Olympics, which, added to his haul from Beijing and Athens, gave him more metal than any Olympian, ever, in any sport. A huge splash, indeed.

The most *surprising* American story? That would be Gabrielle "Gabby" Douglas, who rose to the moment and, when the talc settled, had won an upset gymnastics victory over pre-Olympic favorites Victoria Komova of Russia and U.S.A. teammate Jordyn Weiber to take gold in the Women's Individual All-Around competition.

BRAD PITT

In the end, it wasn't social convention that did it, but lobbying much closer to home. "We're getting a lot of pressure from the kids," Brad Pitt told CBS News of intense campaigning by Maddox, 10, Pax and Zahara, 7, Shiloh, 5 and 3-year-old twins Knox and Vivienne to get mom and dad to tie the knot. "[They say] 'Get Mommy a ring!' Okay, I will, I will." Dad made good on that promise with a monster engagement ring by jeweler Robert Procop ("Brad designed the ring," Procop told PEOPLE; "I helped bring that to fruition") that an independent expert estimated to weigh 10 carats and cost about $1 million.

Change of heart seems to be a recent theme for the couple who once vowed that they would wait to wed until gay marriage was legal everywhere. Days earlier, Angelina's long estranged father, Jon Voight, enjoyed Easter with his grandkids at the couple's Los Angeles home. "I don't think we'll be able to hold out," Pitt said before he presented Angelina with the ring. "It means so much to my kids . . . and it means something to me too, to make that kind of commitment."

JEN & JUSTIN'S LOVE CONNECTION

Friends and fans duly noted when Jennifer Aniston and her guy, Justin Theroux, shifted their home base from a rented apartment to a $21 million Bel Air estate complete with a private vineyard. Were things getting, like, serious? "It's a very exciting time for them," a friend said of Aniston. "They [both] feel ready for whatever the future brings."

The future arrived six months later as the couple celebrated his 41st birthday over a bottle of white in a Manhattan restaurant, and the actor (*Parks and Recreation*) and screenwriter (*Iron Man 2*) popped the question.

Theroux "had an amazing birthday on Friday [Aug. 10]," his rep told PEOPLE exclusively, "receiving an extraordinary gift when his girlfriend, Jennifer Aniston, accepted his proposal of marriage."

"Everyone is really excited for them," a friend says of the couple, whose 15-month courtship spawned a rumor mill—babies! breakups!—that must have sounded familiar to Aniston, whose romances with Vince Vaughn and John Mayer generated similar tabloid fevers. This time, though, was different. "From the beginning Jen's friends thought they were right for each other," a source told PEOPLE. "He treats her like gold, and they just click and complement each other."

As for wedding bells, no date has been set, but pals think marriage and more won't be far off. "Jen loves babies," says one. "They would be great at raising a family together."

Evoking the dangers of centuries past, the *Bounty* sank off North Carolina. Captain Walbridge's decision proved fatal for himself and crewmember Claudene Christian (left).

LOST AT SEA

It was a tragedy from another age. On Oct. 25 (when the size and threat of Hurricane Sandy were well-known) Robin Walbridge, 63, captain of the *Bounty,* a 180-foot, three-masted sailing ship built for the 1962 Marlon Brando film *Mutiny on the Bounty*, took his vessel out of New London, Conn. and set a course south into the Atlantic. Some thought his decision bizarre (Dan Moreland, captain of the tall ship *Picton Castle*, told a reporter, "When I first heard … I thought, 'You've got to be kidding'") but Walbridge believed the *Bounty* was safest in open water and hoped to sail around the worst weather. Responding to skeptics, the HMS Bounty Organization, which ran the ship as a floating museum and seamanship school, said on its Facebook page, "Rest assured that the *Bounty* is safe … *Bounty*'s current voyage is a calculated decision … NOT AT ALL … irresponsible … A SHIP IS SAFER AT SEA THAN IN PORT."

By Sunday night, as seas built, a generator failed and the ship was taking on water. Hours later the organization posted, "Your prayers are needed." After distress calls, the Coast Guard found the *Bounty* early Monday morning, abandoned and sinking, 90 miles off the coast of North Carolina. Fourteen crew members were rescued; the body of another, Claudene Christian, 42, was also recovered. Capt. Walbridge was missing and presumed lost at sea.

CAPTAIN (UN)COURAGEOUS

Madonna, what a mess I've made!" muttered Captain Francesco Schettino, 52, and that may have been his only correct assessment that day. To impress spectators on shore, Schettino had steered his cruise ship, the *Costa Concordia*, off course and too close to the Italian island of Giglio, off Tuscany, where the *Concordia*, with 4,200 passengers aboard, rammed into a rocky outcrop. Even as the boat sank, crew members assured travelers that all was well and suggested they return to their cabins. When the *Concordia* rolled to starboard and partially sank, 32 passengers drowned. By then, though, Captain Schettino had abandoned ship—prompting an exasperated and outraged Coast Guard captain, in a recorded radio communication that became instantly famous, to yell at Schettino to "*Vada a bordo, cazzo!* (Get back on board, for f---'s sake!)." Months later the *Concordia*, awaiting salvage, remains in place, where it's a local tourist attraction.

Captain Schettino, who is expected to face criminal charges, claims he went ashore to oversee the evacuation.

TO SERVE THEM ALL MY DAYS

When Russell Dohner was a boy, he had a terrifying bout of seizures. "When I came out of them, there would always be Dr. Hamilton," he recalls. "I decided I wanted to be like him."

He has done that, with more than a touch of Jimmy Stewart thrown in. As America struggles with medical costs and politicians praise or pillory Obamacare, Dohner, 87, a doctor in Rushville, Ill., does what he has been doing for 57 years: sees all comers in his small office, for the grand and final fee of $5 per visit (up from $2 the day he opened). "That's the way I've always done it," says the gentlemanly bachelor, who lives off income from his farm and draws no salary. "There are quite a few people who come to see me because they can't afford anybody else. I can help." Says patient Mildred Ortiz, 50: "Dr. Dohner works for his patients, and for love."

Dohner has delivered 3,400 babies, works seven days a week and hasn't taken a vacation in 57 years.

TRAYVON MARTIN SHOOTING

While visiting Sanford, Fla., with his father, Trayvon Martin, a 17-year-old Miami Gardens high school honors student, went to a 7-Eleven and bought a can of Arizona Iced Tea and a bag of Skittles. As he headed back to the gated community where his father's girlfriend lives, Trayvon, who was African American, 6'3" and 140 lbs., caught the eye of George Zimmerman, 28, a local crime-watch volunteer who phoned 911. "This guy looks like he's up to no good," Zimmerman said, adding that Trayvon was wearing "a dark hoodie."

What exactly happened between the time Zimmerman called 911 and the moment he fired two bullets from a semiautomatic handgun, one of which fatally struck the teen in the chest, remains unclear. But it is at the heart of a furor that swept the country after local cops, citing Florida's "Stand Your Ground" law, failed to arrest Zimmerman, who claimed he shot Trayvon in self-defense. While the U.S. Justice Department and the FBI launched investigations, supporters held vigils and charges of racism flew, Trayvon's mother, Sybrina Fulton, called for calm. "People want to make this a black and white issue," she told PEOPLE. "But I believe that this is about right and wrong. No one should be shot just because someone else thinks they're suspicious."

While Zimmerman has since been charged by the Florida State Attorney's Office with second degree murder—he is free on bail while awaiting trial—Trayvon's family endures the unbearable. "He really loved his life," Jahvaris Fulton said of his brother Tray. "And now I can't believe he's gone."

"I'm angry, but I think I'm more sad right now," says Trayvon's mom, Sybrina Fulton (with his dad, Tracy Martin, in March).

INSET: Described as "a cop wannabe" who attended a citizens' police academy and phoned police 46 times since August 2004 to report disturbances, Zimmerman quit his job at a mortgage firm and went into hiding after the shooting. Although a friend says, "I'm sure he's not a racist," Zimmerman, who is part Hispanic, is heard on the recording of his 911 call describing Trayvon as "a black man" and saying "These a-holes, they always get away."

1999

2000

2001

FLAT TIRE: The International Cycling Union annulled all seven of Armstrong's Tour de France wins and demanded the return of an estimated $4 million in prize money. Their harsh conclusion? "Lance Armstrong has no place in cycling," said Union president Pat McQuaid. "He deserves to be forgotten."

2003

ET TU, HINCAPIE?

F elix Baumgartner may have jumped with a parachute from 24 miles up (see page 44), but he didn't take 2012's biggest fall. That sad distinction belongs to Lance Armstrong, erstwhile seven-time winner of the Tour de France, who lost all those titles, plus an Olympic bronze medal and all his endorsements and was banned for life from competitive cycling after the United States Anti-Doping Agency concluded he had been at the center of "the most sophisticated, professionalized and successful doping program that sport has ever seen."

For years, Armstrong had aggressively denied he had doped; in August he announced he would no longer fight the charges, calling them a "witch hunt." Eventually, though, the USADA evidence would prove overwhelming: 11 former teammates gave affidavits detailing their own and Armstrong's drug use. For many fans, the final straw came when George Hincapie, a highly respected cyclist who rode at Armstrong's side during all seven Tour wins, admitted that, yes, he and Armstrong had used performance-enhancing drugs.

2002

2004

2005

HOLD THE BUTTER

er Deep-Fried Stuffing on a Stick (five tablespoons of butter; one pound of sausage) wasn't exactly Weight Watchers fare. And the 65-year-old Queen of Comfort Food's infamous Brunch Burger was a belly-buster Elvis would have loved: a hunka hunka ground beef crowned with fried egg and bacon, served on two Krispy Kreme doughnuts. What Food Network star Paula Deen wasn't telling her audience, it turns out, is that she had dropped fatty foods from her *own* grocery list and unplugged her deep fryer after having been diagnosed with Type 2 diabetes in January. Deen chose to reveal her condition only when she simultaneously announced that she would begin endorsing a line of diabetic drugs. "I was surprised by the depth of the hate," she said of critics who perceived her choices to be less than noble. "This is not something I chose. I had been given lemons and I had to try and make lemonade—without sugar!"

DEEP FRIED NO MORE: Deen's healthier diet helped her shed more than 30 lbs. in six months. "I feel a thousand times better," she says. "The whole journey has taught me that I'm stronger than I ever gave myself credit for."

VAMPIRES IN LOVE

———

O nscreen, their chemistry "was electrifying," recalled the director of *Twilight*, the first of the teen passion plays about a girl's love for her undead boyfriend. And fans of the vampire saga swooned when the stars of the film and its blockbuster sequels became real-life, live-in lovers.

Then the three-year romance between Kristen Stewart, 22, and Robert Pattinson, 26—who reigned as Young Hollywood's golden couple—was shattered in July by revelations (in a series of mortifying tabloid photos, below) that the actress had hooked up with Rupert Sanders, the 41-year-old, married-with-kids British director of Stewart's hit *Snow White & the Huntsman*. The scandal drove a stake through the hearts of the franchise's two stars and their fans, as well as Sanders's family. Stewart offered an abject apology, saying in an anguished statement that she had "jeopardized the most important thing in my life, the person I love and respect the most, Rob. I love him, I love him, I'm so sorry." Pattinson, initially, was having none of it. "He's heartbroken and angry," said a friend. "This has been such a blow. Talk about having his heart ripped out."

Ah, but there's resilience in young hearts. According to numerous sources, the pair met up in September and began spending more and more time together. Soon they were a couple again—and Pattinson decided not to sell the L.A. home the pair had shared.

I only have eyes for you: Kim and Kanye in the front row at Paris Fashion Week in July.

WHEN K'S UNITE

———

S eldom are the designs of cupid, and PR, so in sync: In 2012, Kanye West and Kim Kardashian—why doesn't anyone call them K2?—shared a photo-op kind of love.

Your love is taking me higher: The K's rock 'n' roll at Six Flags Magic Mountain in California.

COLORADO BURNING

Wind-whipped into an inferno that roared through drought-parched foothills and consumed suburban split-levels like so much kindling, the Waldo Canyon fire—one of dozens of devastating wildfires that struck the West in the midst of a June heat wave—forced 32,000 residents from their homes and reduced more than 17,000 acres to charcoal. "I hate wind," said a commander of the effort to contain the "astronomically fast" fires that raged around Colorado Springs and Pikes Peak, the inspiration for Katharine Lee Bates's "America the Beautiful" lyrics. "It looks like my house is gone," said one resident to *The New York Times,* who then fled what she called a "volcanic eruption" of flame that engulfed her neighborhood. "It's devastating for all of us."

BIG CHALLENGE: I WANNA BE

NAOMI WATTS AS PRINCESS DI

No question it's enough to make an actress think twice. On the one hand, "The filmmakers came to me, and it's a good script," said actress Naomi Watts of the offer to play Princess Diana. On the other, "It was very scary, and I kind of wanted to say no but I couldn't." The film *Caught in Flight*, due in 2013, focuses on Di's attempts to find love—with Dr. Hasnat Khan and, later, Dodi Al Fayed—and purpose during the last two years of her life. "It is such an honor to be able to play this iconic role—Princess Diana was loved across the world," said Watts. "I look forward to rising to the challenge of playing her onscreen."

AN ICON!

LINDSAY LOHAN AS ELIZABETH TAYLOR

In her first big film in quite a while, Lohan, who mostly had been making headlines for her offscreen exploits, starred as La Liz in a Lifetime network movie, *Liz & Dick*, about the legend's epic and headline-making love affair with, and two marriages to, actor Richard Burton. Although Lohan may not have been the first person most people think of when pondering actresses who resemble Taylor, much can be done with makeup (see above). And the 26-year-old actress argued that she could bring her own experience to the role: "I relate to her on a lot of levels," said Lohan. "Living in the public eye, dealing with the stress of what other people say, whether it's true or not."

DEMI & ASHTON SPLIT

Paramedics who arrived at the film star's sprawling compound in L.A.'s Benedict Canyon on the night of Jan. 23 did not recognize the frail looking and "out of it" woman who, according to a source on the scene, was "shaking, convulsing [and] burning up" after an apparent drug overdose.

"[They] first thought she was a cancer patient who had smoked to relieve her bad symptoms," the source said of Demi Moore, the 49-year-old, age-defying star who was once Hollywood's highest paid actress. "It was panic at the house."

Reeling from the November 2011 breakup of her marriage to Ashton Kutcher, 34, Moore was briefly hospitalized and underwent a month of treatment in a rehab facility.

Long tormented by insecurities about her body and age—"As Demi got older, she convinced herself that she needed to stay young and skinny to remain attractive to her husband," said a source—Moore became increasingly dependent on drugs after her marriage ended and Ashton began dating. "He still cares about [Demi] and wants the best for her," a friend of the *Two and a Half Men* star said. But Moore, whose self-doubts only increased—she told her friend Amanda de Cadenet in *Harper's Bazaar* that what most scares her "is that I'm going to ultimately find out at the end of my life that I'm really not lovable, that I'm not worthy of being loved"—embarked on the frightening spiral that led to her January collapse.

In April, Moore, buoyed by the support of her daughters by Bruce Willis—Rumer, 23, Scout, 20, and Tallulah, 18—and a loyal circle of friends, "looked gorgeous and relaxed," said a guest at a red-carpet event where the actress made her first public appearance since completing treatment. There is still "a lot of work and self-healing to be done," said a source, but Moore appeared to be well on the way to recovery. "She's doing fantastic," said designer Donna Karan, a longtime friend. "She's beautiful."

The couple in 2011. "Demi really wanted to save the marriage but couldn't deal with the pain of his cheating," said a friend of Kutcher's.

Hospitalized in January, Moore seemed, physically, in better form by July.

By year's end, Kutcher was dating his former costar from *That '70s Show*, Mila Kunis.

Despite testimony from eight victims, Sandusky maintained his innocence and blamed his conviction on a "well-orchestrated" conspiracy against him.

COLOSSAL FALL: As the breadth of the scandal became clear, a statue of Joe Paterno, a campus centerpiece and icon of Penn State pride, was draped in a blanket and carted away.

SCANDAL AND CONVICTION

"I'd sometimes scream," said the witness, identified only as Victim 9, as he described being raped by the man he thought was his benefactor, longtime Penn State football assistant coach Jerry Sandusky, 68. Charged with being a sexual predator and serial pedophile who molested young boys—at least one as young as 8 years old—and using a charity he founded to help disadvantaged and troubled teens as a net to lure victims, Sandusky was found guilty in June and sentenced in October to 30 to 60 years in prison. Penn State's legendary head football coach Joe Paterno was fired, along with the university's president and other top officials, for not doing enough to stop Sandusky despite evidence of his crimes. (Paterno died months later). Additionally, the NCAA fined Penn State $60 million and banned the school from bowl competition. "Jerry never gave any sign that this was the kind of man he is," a colleague said of the coach and adoptive father of six once described as Saint Sandusky for his charitable works. "He duped us all."

BULLIED BUS DRIVER

There was no violence, but the video clip was still horrifying: For 10 minutes, a group of 7th graders from a Rochester, N.Y., suburb taunted Karen Klein, a 68-year-old grandmother and school bus monitor, with the cruelest, most vile insults they could conjure. Taken by an unnamed passenger with a cell phone, the video, uploaded to YouTube, went viral in June and received more than 7 million hits.

Within a week, an Internet campaign started by a Canadian who sympathized with Klein raised more than $650,000, enough to allow her to retire and to launch her Karen Klein Anti-Bullying Foundation. "Two wrongs don't make a right," Klein said upon learning that her tormentors—four boys later apologized and were suspended for a year by school officials—had received thousands of death threats. "I'm happy this got out," she said of the video. "Hopefully they'll learn something from this—not just these boys, but all kids."

CELEBS AS **REAL** PEOPLE

From A-list to average Joe: New York artist Danny Evans morphed photos to depict what stars might look like if they'd not found the path to fame, riches and stylists

MILEY CYRUS

JENNIFER ANISTON

RIHANNA

SCARLETT JOHANSSON

BEYONCE

JAY-Z

BRAD PITT

ANGELINA JOLIE

KOURTNEY, KHLOE AND KIM KARDASHIAN, WITH MOM KRIS JENNER

BODY-IN-BAG SENSATION

I SPY A KILLER

▶ Coroner: He could have been victim of poison ▶ Secret agents not ruled out as murder suspects

An inquest video showed that Williams (top, left) couldn't have locked himself in the gym bag.

DEADLY SPY MYSTERY

Any sensible book editor would reject the episode as preposterous. Yet there it was, in jaw-dropping detail, in real life. On Aug. 16, 2010, Gareth Williams, a normally punctilious code breaker for MI6, Britain's spy agency, didn't show up for work. And for a week, his colleagues did nothing. Finally, in response to prompting from his family, police entered his apartment and found the 31-year-old naked and decomposing in a padlocked gym bag in his bathtub. They also found $32,000 worth of designer women's clothing and, on Williams's computer, a history of visiting bondage Web sites. Despite the bizarre circumstances, no one has been able to figure out what happened. A coroner, suggesting that various agencies had bollixed a 21-month investigation, would only say that he had probably died "unlawfully" from poisoning or suffocation. Some speculated that he had been killed by another agency, or even someone inside MI6 (Williams was found to have conducted unauthorized searches on his office computer). Nonetheless, said the coroner, "It is unlikely the death will ever be satisfactorily explained."

FEARLESS FELIX

Sixty-five years to the day after Chuck Yeager became the first human to break the sound barrier, Austrian Felix Baumgartner did the same thing—without a plane. Where Yeager piloted an X-1 rocket plane at supersonic speed, Baumgartner hit Mach 1.24 on Oct. 14 in a "Look, Ma! No wings!" free fall. Wearing a specially designed jump suit, the daredevil 43-year-old former paratrooper rode a 55-story-high helium balloon to an altitude of 128,100 feet. Millions watched via the Internet—the jump was on tape delay in case of disaster—and a support team of engineers, scientists and doctors waited below at a NASA-like mission control center aptly located near Roswell, N.Mex., Baumgartner plummeted from 24 miles up for more than nine minutes, reaching a maximum speed of 833.9 mph before deploying his parachute and landing—on his feet—on terra firma. "It's not about breaking records [and it's] not about getting scientific data," Baumgartner said of information gathered during his jump that would be shared with more traditional future space travelers. "It's all about coming home."

Baumgartner stepped from the balloon's capsule 24 miles up, on Oct. 14 (inset) and, back on Earth nine minutes later, waved to his ground crew.

. . . Angelina Jolie's right leg made a dramatic entrance at the Oscars and hired its own agent (or should have).

2012

THAT WAS THE YEAR THAT ...

. . . Britain's Prince Harry disproved the What Stays in Vegas Theorem, partying happily and heartily (above) until full-frontal nude shots (*not* pictured) surfaced from a game of strip billiards. Despite the predictable media frenzy, the public, for the most part, yawned.

Some stories last just a micromoment yet, somehow, still leave their tiny footprints in the shifting sands of time. These are those stories for 2012

... slackline dancer Andy Lewis made headlines bouncing on a giant rubber band during Madonna's halftime show.

... thanks to Republican presidential hopeful Herman Cain, the phrase "Awwww, shucky ducky!" echoed throughout the land.

... *Home Alone*'s Macaulay Culkin seemed not at all ready for his close-up.

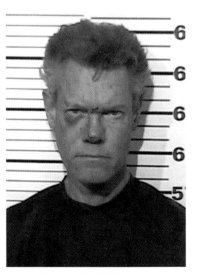

... country star Randy Travis, arrested inebriated and naked in Texas, was *really, really* not ready for his close-up.

... *Fifty Shades of Grey* caused prudes to blush 84 shades of rose.

... *Linsanity*—and dozens of other puns (Lincredible! Linfatuation! It's a Linderella story!) inspired by the rise of out-of-nowhere Knicks phenom Jeremy Lin— rocked the NBA.

. . .*Blossom*'s early '90s dreamboat Joe Lawrence, 36, stripped on The Strip during a three-week gig sharing the stage with the Chippendales dancers in Las Vegas.

. . . retired NBA superstar Shaquille O'Neal earned a PhD in education from Miami's Barry University. "I put in four and a half hard years staying up late at night," O'Neal said. "Of all the things I've done in my life, this is probably my No. 1 accomplishment." Said his proud mom, Lucille: "Now I get to call him Dr. O'Neal!"

THE LIFE OF AN A-LIST TOY

In Manhattan, there's a stuffed baby giraffe who's living the luxe life—but isn't selfish. Everywhere the giraffe goes, she brings along her best bud, Suri Cruise, Katie Holmes and Tom Cruise's 6-year-old daughter. Gymnastics class? Yep. Robert De Niro's Tribeca restaurant Locanda Verde? Of course. Even chopper rides—as every giraffe knows—are always more fun if you share them with a friend.

STAR TRACKS

Brad squints, Julianne Hough plunges, proud
papa Mick Jagger poses, Emma Watson
walks a pink poodle and more: 2012 pix that
captured a moment

BOW SPIRIT

On a Bermuda adventure with beau Ryan Seacrest, actress Julianne Hough took a photogenic flying leap.

SYNCHRONIZED HARRY?

It only *looked* like Prince Harry and Olympic great Usain Bolt were working out a dance routine for *Jamaica's Got Talent*. Actually, Harry was miming Bolt's famous victory pose.

PRINCE BRINGS THE FUNK

Four hundred 11-year-olds in attendance could only hope, someday, to mimic the suave moves Prince Charles threw down at a youth event in the Channel Islands.

YOU LOOKIN' AT *ME*?

"It's kind of like a high school reunion," *Modern Family*'s Ty Burrell said of the PEOPLE/Entertainment Industry Foundation SAG Awards gala, where everyone from the casts of *Glee* and *The Help* to a very relaxed Brad Pitt got into the mellow spirit.

PAPA WAS A ROLLING STONE

Mick Jagger—now 69 and four times a granddad—squired daughters Georgia May (left), 20, and Elizabeth, 28, two of his four children with ex Jerry Hall, at a London photo exhibit marking the Stones' 50th anniversary.

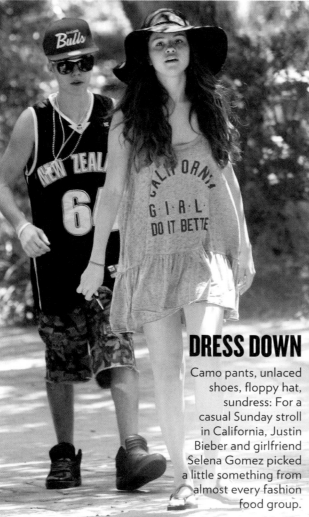

DRESS DOWN

Camo pants, unlaced shoes, floppy hat, sundress: For a casual Sunday stroll in California, Justin Bieber and girlfriend Selena Gomez picked a little something from almost every fashion food group.

HAUTE DOG?

Nope, Darcy the pooch's unusual hue had nothing to do with fashion. "PinkDarcyDog is pink because her owner is raising money for breast cancer," tweeted actress Emma Watson, who took the canine for a stroll in London. "I wish Darcy was my dog, but she isn't."

LIKE DAUGHTER, LIKE DAD?

Katy Perry brought her Elton-esque dad, Keith Hudson, an evangelical pastor, to the premiere of her documentary *Katy Perry: Part of Me* in L.A.

THE LADY IN RED

Shopping in Beverly Hills, a very pregnant Jessica Simpson still managed skyscraper heels.

MEET THE FAM

At home in L.A. with husband Dean McDermott and daughter Hattie, 7 months, Tori Spelling, pregnant with her fourth child, dressed for a dip.

CONTEMPLATION COUTURE

Russell Brand sometimes skirts convention at the West Hollywood yoga studio where he frequently meditates.

BABY, IT'S ME!

Daughter Harper, 7 months, looked as camera-ready as her soccer-star and sometime-model dad, David Beckham, in New York in February.

THE LOVE BOAT?

Taylor Swift seems to have had a longtime crush on all things Kennedy: She pronounced herself "starstruck" after meeting Ethel Kennedy, 84, at the Sundance Film Festival, and has said her style is inspired by Ethel and Jackie Kennedy. So perhaps it shouldn't have come as a *complete* surprise that she and Robert F. Kennedy's grandson Conor, 18, became an item and were photographed sailing off the coast of Massachusetts, looking a lot like another famous couple in 1953 (inset). Come fall, though, with Kennedy back in prep school and Swift releasing a new album, the couple reportedly called it a day.

TINY TINA?

30 Rock's Tina Fey took look-alike daughter Alice, 6, to an event at the Four Seasons in Beverly Hills in January.

THAT'S AMOUR

On a fine summer day, a multitasking Mary-Kate Olsen 26 (left), strolled in Manhattan with her new guy, banker Olivier Sarkozy, 43 (half brother of former French president Nicolas Sarkozy), and his daughter Margot.

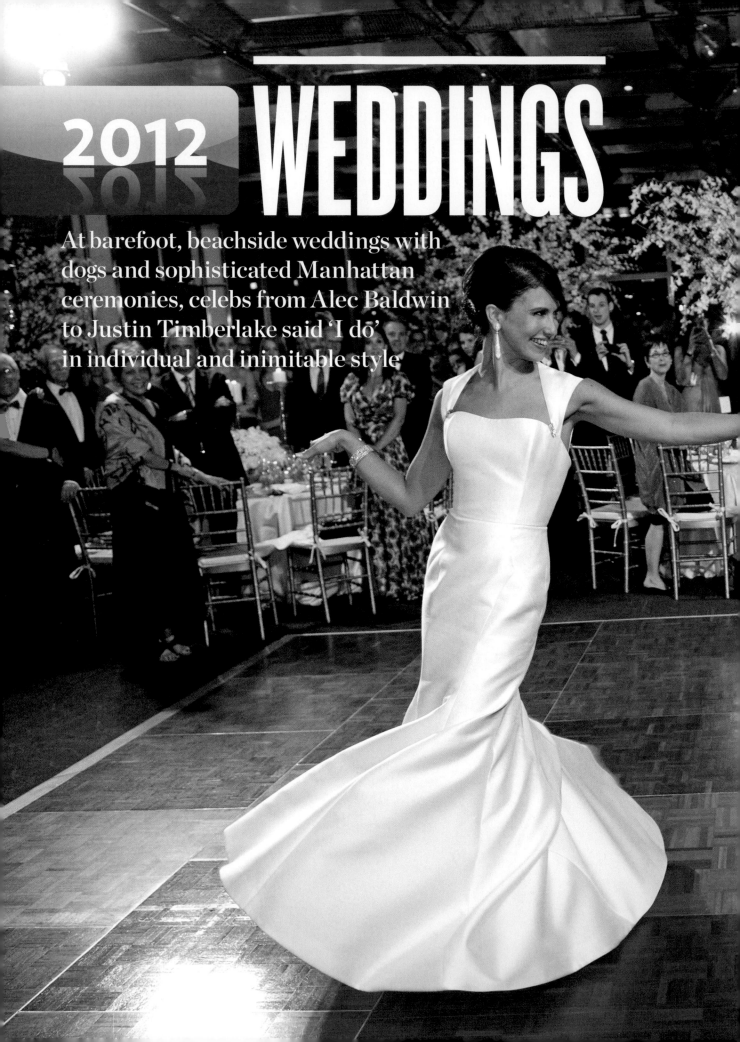

2012 WEDDINGS

At barefoot, beachside weddings with dogs and sophisticated Manhattan ceremonies, celebs from Alec Baldwin to Justin Timberlake said 'I do' in individual and inimitable style

ALEC BALDWIN
—
HILARIA THOMAS

Sometimes you get lucky. As Hilaria Thomas recalls that fateful day in 2011, she was dining at a Manhattan restaurant and "I literally said, 'Universe, I'm ready to fall in love.' And my girlfriend said, 'Hilaria, shut up. Alec Baldwin is looking at you!'" The two began talking and, yada yada yada, on June 30, Thomas, 28, who co-owns a yoga studio, and the two-time Emmy-winning *30 Rock* star were married at St. Patrick's Old Cathedral in New York City. "Marriage is made for you to make a commitment to someone who is worth it," says Baldwin, 54. "And I met someone who is worth it."

RYAN REYNOLDS
—
BLAKE LIVELY

Once they began dating in 2011, things moved quickly. By November, they were visiting her family in Utah; near Christmas, it was his clan in Vancouver. "They knew early on this was it," says an L.A. source. And they were right: On Sept. 9, Lively, 25, and Reynolds, 35, who first met while costarring in *The Green Lantern* in 2010, wed in an elegant but hush-hush ceremony at the Boone Hall Plantation & Gardens outside Charleston, S.C.

The bride wore a couture Marchesa ball gown with hand-draped silk tulle bodice with crystal and rose gold embroidery; the groom opted for a Burberry suit and custom leather suspenders. They vowed to "support and love each other and to make each other laugh," says a witness. "The whole time they were beaming." After the I do's and wining, dining and dancing, the couple had one more surprise in store for guests: 35 illuminated (but biodegradable!) "wish lanterns" lifted gently from a riverside dock into the night sky. "It was one of the most beautiful things I have ever seen in my life," says an onlooker. "When they rose in the air, everyone cheered. It was a happy moment."

MATTHEW McCONAUGHEY
—
CAMILA ALVES

There are weddings, and there are Texas weddings. "Everyone was calling it glamping—like glam camping," said one guest of the 47 air-conditioned tents erected on the happy couple's Austin estate, where 120 guests, including Reese Witherspoon, Kenny Chesney and Woody Harrelson, spent three days and two nights celebrating. "It was like a cool commune." With, like many communes, a spiritual purpose: After six years together and two children, son Levi, 4, and daughter Vida, 2 1/2, "We decided to embrace the ritual of marriage as an opportunity and adventure we'll take together," said McConaughey, 42. Said the 29-year-old Alves, a Brazilian-born model and designer: "Levi has asked many times over the years, 'Mama, why am I a McConaughey but you aren't?' They are both very excited. Somehow they both seem to understand what we are doing on a spiritual level."

DREW BARRYMORE
—
WILL KOPELMAN

For the adults, there was a great ceremony and gourmet food; for kids, a teepee, pillows, blankets and a mini movie theater playing *Pippi Longstocking* and *Finding Nemo*. "The day was perfect," said the pregnant Barrymore of her June 2 wedding to art consultant Will Kopelman, 34, in Montecito, Calif. "Everyone we love and care about was there. It was as fun and meaningful as we ever could have hoped."

"Anne looked very, very happy all night," a friend says of the bride. "She got what she wanted: a beautiful, regular wedding with no movie star glitz."

ANNE HATHAWAY

—

ADAM SHULMAN

Flowers in Mason jars, and a Valentino gown; I do's under a redwood tree, and a six-carat engagement ring: Hathaway and her beau of three years combined homey and glam at their September wedding on a private ranch overlooking the Pacific near Big Sur, Calif. But down to the planks bearing the couple's favorite phrases about love and marriage that marked the path to the wedding site, "Everything came from the heart," says a Hathaway friend. "It was breathtaking." Said another: "Adam is incredibly warm. He's all 'love, peace and happiness.' Annie is like that too."

Hathaway, 29, must have recognized that from the start. "I was actually looking forward to a little alone time, and then I fell in love like a fool!" she told *Marie Claire U.K* of meeting Shulman, 31, an actor, in '08. Valentnio, 80, who designed her gown and a slinky tea-length dress she wore later, came out of retirement to create the dresses for Hathaway, a friend. He did it "with great affection," said his partner Giancarlo Giammetti, "thinking about a happy bride—happy to marry the right man."

WYNONNA JUDD
—
CACTUS MOSER

"It's a miracle," said the twice-divorced Judd, 48, of finding love with Moser, 55, a musician she has known for decades. "I've been alone in the wilderness for years. You wonder, 'Is there life after all the crap I've been through?' And the answer is 'abso-stinkin'-lutely!'"

RICKI LAKE

CHRISTIAN EVANS

Planning for a big wedding but freaking about managing the guest list, Lake, 43, and Evans, 40, a jewelry designer, went small—*really* small: The pair exchanged self-created vows before a handful of friends and their dogs Jeffie and Pacha at a beachside ceremony in Montecito, Calif., that, says Lake, "was just for us."

MARK ZUCKERBERG
—
PRISCILLA CHAN

"Billions or no, they've always stayed down-to-earth," said a friend of the Facebook founder Zuckerberg and Chan, his steady of nine years and a recent medical school grad. The day after their May 19 wedding, both changed their Facebook statuses to "married."

ENGAGED

MILEY CYRUS
—
LIAM HEMSWORTH

She shared her first kiss with him, on camera, in the 2010 film *The Last Song*; in May, the former *Hanna Montana* star and Aussie actor, 22, who costarred in *The Hunger Games*, became engaged. So far, she's got a 3.5-carat cushion-cut Neil Lane diamond, but, at press time, the couple hadn't set a date.

JUSTIN TIMBERLAKE
JESSICA BIEL

The bridesmaids wore white; the bride herself, thinking "romance, romance, romance," wore pink and was, says her groom, "the most beautiful thing I have ever seen." As for how they pulled off the elegant and private ceremony, at the Borgo Egnazi resort in Puglia, Italy: "We really did this whole thing together," says Timberlake, 31. "She did the soup and I did the nuts. And that we didn't kill each other, that's a bonus!" After five years together, why now? "It's as simple as having someone there to open up that pickle jar," says Biel, 30, "and as complicated as deciding to be in each other's lives forever."

Yessir, that's my baby: Beyoncé and Jay-Z, Jessica Simpson, Kristin Cavallari, Snooki and more celebrate little newcomers

J.R. MARTINEZ

DIANA GONZALEZ-JONES

He's an Iraq war veteran, a fan-fave *Dancing with the Stars* winner and, now, a mushball dad. "I kiss her nonstop all day long," says J.R. Martinez of daughter Lauryn Annabelle. "I just want to keep holding her." And, he adds, he's discovering new things every day. "I was raised by a single mother," says Martinez. "So I'm learning what a father is supposed to say. Looking at Belle, I feel like she's going to teach me a lot."

JESSICA SIMPSON

ERIC JOHNSON

When 9-lb. 13-oz. Maxwell Drew arrived via cesarean, one nurse exclaimed, "Whoa! She is a chunk!" And, immediately, the recipient of big love: "My life completely changed," said Simpson, 31. "She's my career at the moment." For now, vanity is out the window. "I'm less concerned about how my hair looks or if my gut is showing," said Simpson, who, at first, breast-fed every three hours, like clockwork: "It is the first time I've every kept to a schedule in my life!" Fiancé Eric Johnson, 32, said it best, says Simpson: "'When Maxwell was born, it felt like we were born again.'"

JACKSON RATHBONE

SHEILA HAFSADI

In the *Twilight Saga*, he plays Jasper Hale, a vampire who can read others' emotions. But nothing prepared Rathbone, 27, for the "deep and profound love" he would feel for baby Monroe Jackson Rathbone VI—a.k.a. Roe—born July 5 to girlfriend Sheila Hafsadi. The actor met the burlesque dancer, 24, at a Florida club; within three months, they were expecting. Still, they say, they slipped fairly easily into their new roles. "I am captain of the diapers," says Rathbone. And vampire experience is clearly a plus: "I'm still up pretty late with this guy. "

SNOOKI

JIONNI LAVALLE

Some things don't change: In the delivery room, "before I was pushing, I put bronzer on and [false] eyelashes," says Snooki of prepping for the arrival of baby Lorenzo Dominic LaValle on Aug. 26. "I wanted to look pretty for him." But the *Jersey Shore* star—currently living with fiancé Jionni LaValle at his parents' home—says her wildest days are over: "I have no intention of going to a club. I'm over it. I'd rather stay home with our son—that's fun." That said, her wedding, still in the planning stages, will have the Snooki touch: "I'll wear something sparkling, blingy and white," she says, "And my bridesmaids will wear leopard print."

KRISTIN CAVALLARI AND JAY CUTLER

You might not have known it from her bad-girl roles on *Laguna Beach* and *The Hills,* but Kristin Cavallari always dreamed of having a family. "I just didn't imagine being a mom this young," says the reality star, 25. But after 7-lb. 9-oz. Camden Jack arrived on Aug. 8, Cavallari tweeted, "Being a mom is the most incredible feeling. I am so in love with this little boy!" Now Cavallari says that she and her Chicago Bears quarterback fiancé, Jay Cutler, 29, are just getting started. "Jay wants four kids," says Cavallari, who hasn't set a wedding date yet but has a plan. "I can see us having another baby in a year, but I definitely want Camden walking down our aisle first!"

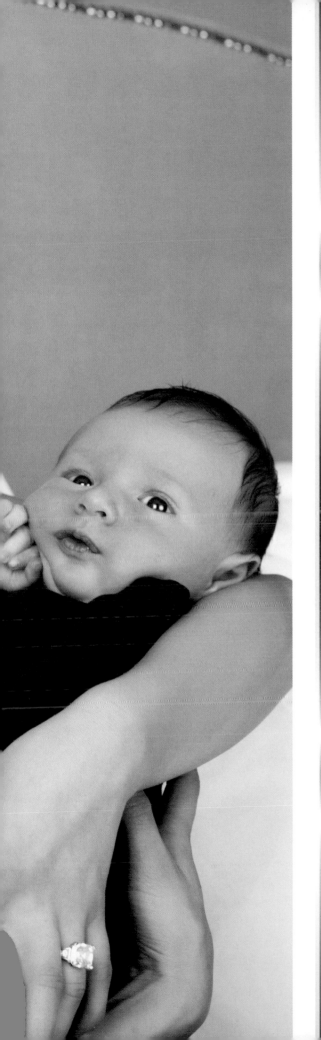

JAY-Z AND BEYONCE

"Her birth was emotional, extremely peaceful; we are in heaven," Beyoncé and husband Jay-Z said in a statement shortly after the arrival of daughter Blue Ivy Carter on Jan. 7. "It was the best experience of both of our lives." Five months later, nothing had changed: "I just stare at her all day," Beyoncé told PEOPLE. "She is my favorite thing in the world, and my No. 1 job is to protect her."

2012 SPLITS

Katy Perry and Russell Brand; Johnny Depp and Vanessa Paradis; Heidi and Seal; Danny DeVito and Rhea Perlman! Among celebs, 2012 may be remembered as The Great Parting

KATY PERRY

—

RUSSELL BRAND

Sigh. It started with such promise. "I threw a bottle straight at him," Perry told *Esquire* of an early encounter with Brand. "Hit him smack dab on the head. Can you imagine the horrible feeling he had, when he was used to getting everything he wanted?" Love followed quickly, and intensely. "I'm like, 'Oh my God! I am you! You are me!'" said Perry. "[We are] two divas in one house . . . It's like splitting the atom: It shouldn't happen."

True that, apparently: Despite a glamorous four-day Indian wedding that featured a tiger photo-safari and two elephants named Laxmi and Mala, the marriage flamed out after 14 months. Friends blamed time apart and different lifestyles: Perry liked to party; Brand, a recovering alcohol and sex addict, shunned nightlife. It probably didn't help that, left alone, he palled around with other women. "Russell needs constant reassurance that he's funny and engaging," says a source from his film *Rock of Ages*. "When she wasn't around he thrived on female companionship, romantic or not." All in all, it was not a recipe for success: Ultimately, "it just cooled off. And when it did, they realized there wasn't anything to stay married for."

HEIDI KLUM

SEAL

They were a glam couple given to big gestures and prominent PDA. When Seal proposed in 2004, he did it in an igloo adorned with rose petals and a bearskin rug atop a 14,000-ft. high glacier in British Columbia. Over the years, parties included an '80s-themed get-together, a masquerade ball and a Venetian-inspired bash in 2011 where, a friend of Klum's later recalled, "they were kissing and holding hands and laughing the whole time. There were no signs they were having problems."

But even then, says another Klum friend, trouble loomed: "They were just really great at keeping it private and putting on that 'perfect couple' front that everyone expected." Which is why it came as a jolt to most friends and fans when the *Project Runway* host and the singer announced in January they were splitting. "Just shocking," said pal Jason Binn. "I've only seen them as the most loving couple."

Friends blame time apart, particularly the months Seal spent on a European tour in late 2011. Said someone who knows them both: "It got harder and harder for them to re-engage in the relationship after being apart for so long." A Christmas vacation in Aspen left them feeling "more lows than highs," said one friend. "They realized while they love each other, they're not in love anymore."

JENNIE GARTH

PETER FACINELLI

It was an intense love," says Garth, looking back. "Did I think we'd be the old couple walking hand-in-hand down the beach? Yes, I wanted that." The former *90210* star and Facinelli, also an actor, met in 1995 on the set of the TV movie *An Unfinished Affair*. Nine months later, she became pregnant with their first child, Lucia, though the couple didn't marry for another five years. "I wanted him to want to get married," she says. "He didn't want to until then, and I was fine with that." What went wrong after 16 years together? Facinelli, approached by People, declined to comment. Says Garth: "There were the common issues any woman has, especially a woman in this industry of insecurities. There was jealousy over having to see your husband onscreen with another woman. It wasn't always easy."

Another possible factor was his recent success in the *Twilight* series and the cable series *Nurse Jackie*. "He deserves to do with that success whatever he wants to do with it," she says. "I'm not sure what it is that he's looking for right now. I don't even know if he knows. Did he change? You'd have to ask him. We want different things now."

JOHNNY DEPP
—
VANESSA PARADIS

Clearly, something was wrong. On the night of the Paris premiere of *The Rum Diary*—produced by and starring Depp—Paradis, his lover of nearly 14 years and mother of his two children—went to a concert instead. The following May, when she skipped that Cannes Film Festival screening of the latest *Pirates of the Caribbean* sequel, it was clear the couple were kaput. "They bet they could move to California and be on long stays on film locations for his career . . . and that things would continue there as they had in the south of France," says a source close to the couple. "They lost that bet. Vanessa went . . . several years between film projects, while he became Jack Sparrow."

AMY POEHLER

—

WILL ARNETT

Say it ain't so: On Sept. 6, Amy Poehler and Will Arnett, both stars of popular NBC sitcoms (*Parks and Recreation* for her; *Up All Night* for him), announced they were separating after nine years of marriage. "They've been apart for months," a source close to the couple told PEOPLE. The devoted parents of Archie, 4, and Abel, 2, "used to sneak away for date nights with friends at the Chateau [Marmont]," says the source, but the long hours on the set eventually took a toll: "Will and Amy have a lot of love for each other. It just wasn't working anymore."

KOBE BRYANT
—
VANESSA BRYANT

Vanessa, 29, filed to end her 10-year union with the NBA star, 33, on Dec. 16, 2011. She famously stuck by Bryant—with whom she has two daughters, Natalia, 8, and Gianna, 5—when he was accused of rape in 2003. (The criminal case was later dropped.) No word on the fate of the $4 million "apology" ring he gave his wife that year.

DANNY DEVITO
—
RHEA PERLMAN

And the world shifted slightly on its axis: After 30 years of marriage, 42 years living together, three grown children and decades of being cited as an example that, yes, Virginia, celebrity marriages *can* last, actors Danny DeVito, 67, and his wife, Rhea Perlman, 64, confirmed in October they were separating. Professionally, the diminutive couple—at 5'1", Perlman towers over DeVito by an inch—thrived as outsiders; both won sitcom Emmys playing tough, wisecracking working stiffs (he as Louie, the dispatcher on *Taxi*; she as *Cheers* waitress Carla). They also cofounded the production company Jersey Films, known for *Pulp Fiction* and *Erin Brockovich*. No reason was given for the split, and a source said no third parties were involved: "There's nothing scandalous."

RUSSELL CROWE
—
DANIELLE SPENCER

They'll always have Woolloomooloo. It was clear that the couple's nine-year marriage, much of it spent in that Sydney, Australia, neighborhood, had hit the rocks when Spencer, 43, stepped out *sans* wedding ring—and on the arm of her Down Under *Dancing with the Stars* partner. Crowe, 48, who had been on film sets most the year and was touring with his band in New York City when the split became public, tweeted that everyone at his latest concert "missed the girl from Rose Bay," where the couple had bought a home in 2011.

2012 MOVIES

Vampires, superheroes and a bat ruled the box office; Hollywood loved Uggie; and all the CSI in the world couldn't save *Battleship* from a watery grave. Blub.

THE HUNGER GAMES

With Harry Potter retired and vampires in their twilight, Suzanne Collins's dystopian tale of starving children forced to hunt each other for the sake of cultural entertainment staked its claim as next great film trilogy—and grossed more than $680 million.

THE AVENGERS

The international language isn't Esperanto, it's Special Effects. Filmdom's fab four—Iron Man, Captain America, the Hulk and Thor—team up to save (and lure) the world, grossing more than $1.5 billion.

TWILIGHT

"The room shorted out, the sky opened up, and I was like, 'This is going to be good!'" Catherine Hardwicke, director of 2008's *Twilight,* recalls of the first time she auditioned Kristen Stewart (Bella) and Robert Pattinson (Edward) together. Five films—including this year's finale, *Breaking Dawn: Part 2*—billions of dollars and millions of fluttering female hearts confirmed that Hardwicke's instinct was spot-on.

BATMAN

Clearly, there's more than one way to film a bat. The '60s TV *Batman* was pure camp (Thwock! Wham! Pow!); the '80s -'90s film versions offered big stars (Clooney, Schwarzenegger, Nicholson) and went well enough with popcorn. But director Christopher Nolan's dark, fully imagined trilogy, starring a perfectly cast Christian Bale and brought to a satisfying conclusion with 2012's *The Dark Knight Rises,* redefined the franchise and set an almost impossible new standard: From now on, Bruce Wayne–wannabes will have to think long and hard before stepping up to bat.

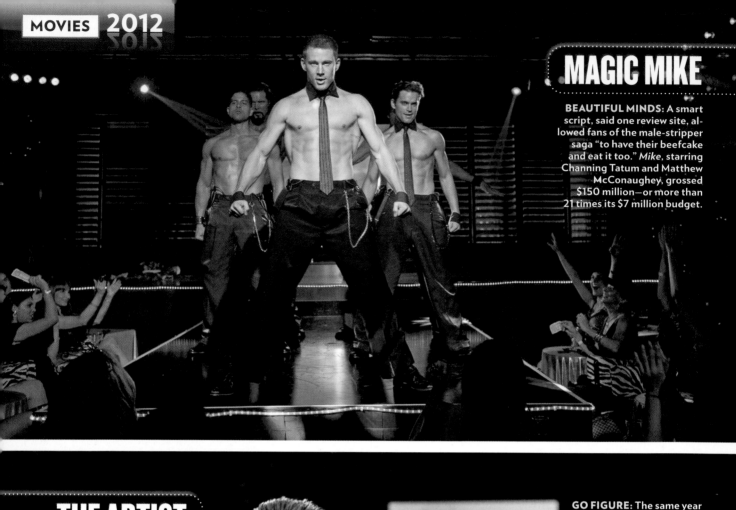

MAGIC MIKE

BEAUTIFUL MINDS: A smart script, said one review site, allowed fans of the male-stripper saga "to have their beefcake and eat it too." *Mike*, starring Channing Tatum and Matthew McConaughey, grossed $150 million—or more than 21 times its $7 million budget.

THE ARTIST

GO FIGURE: The same year that gave us *The Avengers* saw the Academy Awards for Best Picture, Best Director (Michel Hazanavicius) and Best Actor (Jean Dujardin) go to a silent, black-and-white film about a guy, a girl and a dog.

TED

Everybody doesn't like something, but lots of people, it seems, have a soft spot for a cheerfully obscene talking teddy bear. A mockable premise turned in to a megahit for writer-director Seth MacFarlane and star Mark Wahlberg.

DOUBLES FEATURED

A raft of late-2012 biopics—*Hitchcock*; *Lincoln*, from director Steven Spielberg; and *Hyde Park on the Hudson*, about the character and love life of Franklin Delano Roosevelt on the eve of World War II—challenged actors to channel icons.

Honest Abe and . . .

. . . ersatz Abe, Daniel Day-Lewis

Bill Murray . . .

. . . as Franklin Roosevelt

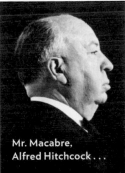

Mr. Macabre, Alfred Hitchcock . . .

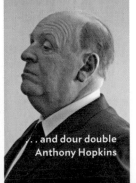

. . . and dour double Anthony Hopkins

SLAMMED AT THE CINEPLEX

JOHN CARTER

Despite a $250 million budget, a stellar pedigree (*Finding Nemo*'s Andrew Stanton directed) and the best names since *Star Wars*—Barsoom! Sab Than! Jeddak of Zodanga!—the interplanetary tale of Therns and Tharks landed with a thud.

ROCK OF AGES

Or *Rock of Aged*? Neither their peers nor their peers' progeny, it turns out, wanted to see Tom Cruise, 49, Alec Baldwin, 54, and Catherine Zeta-Jones, 42, in a movie about the bombastic glories of the hair-band era.

BATTLESHIP

Taylor Kitsch starred in *John Carter* (see above) *and* this alien-invasion flop, making the 31-year-old actor—who also appeared in 2006's *Snakes on a Plane*—the most snake-bit actor of 2012.

DOWNTON ABBEY

After winning several Emmys and an obsessive audience in its debut season, the *Masterpiece* import about a British manor house exploded into a phenomenon so big that PBS began being compared to HBO. The romantic ups and downs of Lady Mary and her distant cousin Matthew, the refined drop-dead sarcasm of Maggie Smith, the murder charge against Lord Grantham's valet—the show was the perfect blend of highbrow taste and low gossip. The news that Shirley MacLaine would appear in season 3 was hailed by fans as if the *Titanic* had been resurrected.

2012 TV

The year's breakout hits found viewers embracing both a veddy British period drama and a reality show that would have embarrassed *The Beverly Hillbillies*; Elizabeth II jumped from Olympic heights; the hottest new comedy was about sex and the borough of Brooklyn; and Clint Eastwood talked to a chair

British refinement, soap opera plot: Paralyzed by a war wound, Matthew miraculously rose from his wheelchair and proposed to his true love Lady Mary (Michelle Dockery)—but only after, of course, his inconvenient fiancée died suddenly during the Spanish influenza epidemic.

HERE COMES HONEY BOO BOO

Cheesiest hit? TLC's reality show about beauty doll Alana Thompson and her rural Southern family. If you hear "recognize" pronounced "redneckonize," blame her.

BREAKING BAD

In its final season, AMC's nasty cult hit about a nerd-slash-druglord (Bryan Cranston) suddenly had massive buzz as audiences caught up with On-Demand and DVD.

HOMELAND

See something … wait, *did* you see something? In Showtime's great drama, mentally ill CIA agent Claire Danes suspects war hero Damian Lewis is a terrorist.

The London summer Olympics on NBC had the most watched and certainly most talked-about opening ceremony ever. Here's why: In one partly prefilmed gag, 007 (Daniel Craig) escorted an unsmiling Elizabeth II into a helicopter—then her stunt double parachuted into the stadium. The night also featured a giant Lord Voldemort and dancing nurses. But the Queen stole the show. Cheeky thing.

HER MAJESTY'S PUBLIC SERVICE

What was *that*? *Mad Men* actress Jessica Paré's full-tilt sex kitten rendition of an obscure song sparked a million water-cooler conversations the next morning—and probably a zillion Google searches. The answer: "Zou Bisou Bisou" (rough translation: "Oh! Kiss Kiss") was a French hit in 1962.

WHAT'S NEW PUSSYCAT!

GOP CHAIR MAN

Clint Eastwood's speech at the Republican Convention was a classic—of some kind: He taunted a chair, pretending it was the President. If this seemed eccentric, the 82-year-old icon later said, tough: "One advantage of being my age is that, you know, what can they do to ya?"

NO. 1 WITH A BULLET

Family feuds are bad for bloodlines, but they can be good for business. Six hours long and littered with corpses, History's *Hatfields & McCoys* was the No. 1-rated entertainment telecast in ad-supported cable history: an average 13.8 million viewers over three nights. It also sparked a comeback for Kevin Costner, who won an Emmy as Devil Anse Hatfield.

LENA, GROWNUP

Having made one art-house film, 26-year-old Lena Dunham (above left) overnight found herself TV's brightest new voice, hailed as some rare amalgam of Tina Fey, Louis C.K. and Zooey Deschanel. *Girls*, the HBO show she created and starred in, was widely praised as a grittier descendant of *Sex and the City* moved from Manhattan to Brooklyn and with sensible shoes replacing Jimmy Choos. After a big-bang 10-episode start, *Girls'* second season is set to premiere in January 2013. (No pressure, Lena!)

HELLO AND GOODBYE

After nearly a year and nearly 60 cohosts, Kelly Ripa finally (drumroll!) chose the man to replace dear departed Regis Philbin: former NFL star Michael Strahan.

SUNSET AT SUNRISE

With the once-dominant *Today* show's ratings slipping, cohost of one year Ann Curry lost her job. She went peacefully, if not happily. "I'm sorry I couldn't carry the ball to the finish line," she wept, "but, man, I did try."

2012

MUSIC

One Direction went only up; Fun. was; Adele rolled in the Grammys; and YouTubers went nuts for the Gangnam stylings of a guy named Psy

More fun than a bag o' Biebers?
One Direction heartthroblets
(clockwise from top, left)
Niall Horan, Zayn Malik,
Louis Tomlinson, Harry Styles,
and Liam Payne.

ONE DIRECTION

Lo, once there was the Monkees.
And New Edition. And New Kids on
the Block, Boyz II Men, Backstreet
Boys, 'N Sync, Hanson and the
Jonas Brothers. Now cometh,
with cute hairstyles and even
cuter Harry Styles, One Direction
(Scream! Squeal! Sob! Faint!), the
Brit-born boy band *du jour*, or *de
l'année*, whose debut album *Up All
Night* sold over 3 million copies and
set young hearts aflutter
from Liverpool to Lhasa.

Another song that will forever make you think of 2012? "Somebody That I Used To Know" by Australia's Wouter De Backer, far better known by his stage name, Gotye (pronounced "GO-tee-yay").

FUN.

GOTYE

EVERYBODY UP!: No matter what you call it—alternative power-pop graduation anthem, anyone?—the oddly punctuated band's megahit, "We Are Young," was just plain fun, period.

ADELE

CARLY RAE JEPSEN

KEEP IT ROLLING: The British wonder took home six Grammys, including Song of the Year for "Rolling in the Deep." But the best was yet to come: Her first child, a son, was born on Oct. 19.

Sure, the most ubiquitous hit of the year, Jepson's "Call Me Maybe," sold more than 10 million copies and launched YouTube versions by everyone from Justin Bieber (above) to the U.S. Olympic Swim Team. But the real mark of success? When former Secretary of State Colin Powell sang a few bars on *CBS This Morning*.

PSY

The Macarana on steroids. South Korean pop star Psy's epically goofy song-and-dance video "Gangnam Style" sparked more than half-a-billion YouTube hits, countless parodies and a *Saturday Night Live* appearance for the surprised singer.

2012 FASHION

Red carpet wows, epic flubs, trends of the year— and Hollywood's hottest septuagenarian!

FLASH BAIT

Sure, it was the year of crazy pants and peplums, dramatic nail art and even (shades of Sonny Bono!) fluffy fake-fur vests. And we'll always have Snooki. But given the right time and place—say, a red carpet in Cannes, packed with paparazzi, in May— old-school elegance, boosted by a soupçon of Hollywood glam, is hard to beat. Eva Longoria, in a gown by Marchesa, got the recipe right.

CARPET BAGGERS

It was time to wear a gown, and they didn't clown around: These six looks stole the show on red carpets from Venice to Beverly Hills. What made the difference? A little sparkle, a little peek-a-boo and, in Sofia Vergara's case, perhaps a Little Mermaid.

CHARLIZE THERON
In Dior Haute Couture, Golden Globes, Beverly Hills

BLAKE LIVELY
In Zuhair Murad, *Savages* premiere, L.A.

MICHELLE WILLIAMS
In Louis Vuitton, the Academy Awards, L.A.

ZOE SALDANA
In Prabal Gurung, CFDA Fashion Awards, New York City

SOFIA VERGARA
In Vera Wang, Golden Globes, Beverly Hills

KATE HUDSON
In Atelier Versace, Venice Film Festival

101

WORST DRESSED

When celebrities make dramatic fashion choices, who protects the innocent bystanders?

ERIN WASSON
I ran through the car wash to get here!

SARAH JESSICA PARKER
Ready for bed. At a quaint New England B&B. In, oh, 1873?

FERGIE
And from the Victoria's Secret Halloween catalog . . .

DO THE VICTORIA!

Y ou put your left foot in/ You jut your right hip out/ Stare blankly with your eyeballs/ As you make a little pout! Victoria Beckham strikes a pose, frequently.

JOHNNY WEIR
For those who thought Liberace just never took it quite *far* enough

JANE, NOT PLAIN

O nce upon a time, not long ago, this was not what 75 looked like. Actually, even now, it's not what 75 looks like. But it *is* what Jane Fonda, who turned three score and fifteen on Dec. 21, 2012, looks like (she was photographed at Cannes Film Festival in May). Of course, not everyone has her genes. Or dedication to exercise. ("It's like the number one ingredient for successful aging," she said on *Today*. "It makes a difference for all aspects of your life and your body.") And not everyone would make, as she did, the choice to have plastic surgery. ("This year I got tired of not looking like how I feel, and I wanted a more refined chin line like I used to have," Fonda blogged in 2010, when she had work done "on my chin and neck and had the bags taken away from under my eyes.") But whatever the alchemy, there's one fact that's beyond debate: This is Jane Fonda at 75.

5 X 2012

A quintet of trends that, next year, will cause your friends to say, "Whoa, brontosaurus! That is so 2012!"

Emma Watson

2

NAIL ART!

It's a party at your fingertips. Or, more precisely, on your fingertips. At last, fashion goes digital!

Zooey Deschanel

Heidi Klum

3

PEPLUMS!

A skirt for your skirt! Flatters the waist! Bonus: One of the three best words in fashion (see also: "dirndl" and "snood")!

4

STATEMENT NECKLACES!

They're big! They're bold! They build stupendous neck muscles!

Sandra Bullock

Camila Alves

Padma Lakshmi

Kristen Stewart

1

CRAZY PANTS!

Dyed, painted, printed. Anything but plain. A "look at me" look (but really— aren't they all?)

5

COLORBLOCK!

Minimal detail, maximum tint. You too can look like a Mondrian painting in heels!

DAVY JONES

Baby-boomers need no explanation; for anyone who does: Davy Jones was your parent's Justin Bieber. In 1965 the 17-year-old Brit, already a Tony nominee on Broadway for his portrayal of the Artful Dodger in *Oliver!*, answered a casting ad seeking "a quartet of hip, insane folk-oriented rock 'n' rollers." The four winners—Jones, Micky Dolenz, Peter Tork and Michael Nesmith—became the Monkees, stars of a kid's TV show and, overnight, a pop sensation whose albums—including four No. 1's in one year—briefly outsold the Beatles and Rolling Stones (the band even boasted Jimi Hendrix as an opening act). "The show made me a sex symbol," said Jones, the most crush-worthy of the quartet. "Not that fans wanted to take me home to bed; they wanted to hang my poster on their wall."

When the Monkees broke up in the early '70s, Jones entered a long stretch in the showbiz and psychological wilderness: "I was depressed," he told PEOPLE in 1992. "I became a walking wild man, meeting two, three girls a day. I didn't know how to live." Married for the third time in 2009, he was still performing regularly and loved spending time with horses—a passion for Jones, who had briefly trained as a jockey before becoming a Monkey. The morning before he died, of a heart attack at 66, he had just been out for a quick ride. Said his daughter Talia: "He went out doing what he loved."

2012 FAREWELL

In 2012 family and fans mourned the loss of Andy Griffith, Donna Summer, Nora Ephron, Neil Armstrong, Gore Vidal, the Beastie Boys' Adam Yauch and many more

Sand simians (clockwise from top): Monkees Davy Jones, Micky Dolenz, Peter Tork and Michael Nesmith in 1967. "Dave was great to hang with," Said Dolenz. "He was the go-to guy for having fun."

NORA EPHRON

—

She lived life, even the painful parts, on the page, and you had to laugh. The betrayal she felt when a sixth-grade friend outpaced her in the training-bra race (see the 1972 essay "A Few Words About Breasts"). The way she rallied when, weeks after giving birth, she was among the last to know her second husband was cheating (see *Heartburn*). The harsh dating truths—when someone's not that attractive, they're always described as "having a good personality"—she mulled during her single years (see *When Harry Met Sally...*). But when Ephron—author, observer, screenwriter, director—entered her final battle with cancer, she told almost no one outside her immediate family; her death, at 71, caught friends, including Tom Hanks, Meryl Streep and Steve Martin off guard. Her speciality, her friends suggested, was sharing joy, which may explain why she had no time for tearful farewells. "It was her sense of wanting to live," said her friend Cynthia McFadden, "until she didn't."

DONNA SUMMER

Put the records on—"Love to Love You Baby," "Hot Stuff," "She Works Hard for the Money," "Last Dance"— and those old platform shoes in your closet might start doing the Hustle all by themselves. As a definer of the era, Disco Queen Donna Summer ranks rights up there with the Bee Gees and ahead of bell-bottoms and mirrored disco balls. After the glitter faded, and following a difficult divorce and custody battle, Summer fought depression and a prescription drug problem before becoming a born-again Christian. In the end, she hid her struggle with lung cancer from all but family and a few close friends. "She handled it like a soldier," says her best friend, author Alice Harris. "She didn't want to burden anyone."

MIKE WALLACE

In 1962, after the death of his son Peter, 19, in a mountain climbing accident, journalist Mike Wallace had an epiphany. "I knew that the only work I'd do for the rest of my life would be . . . serious, substantive journalism," he said. "I wanted to do something . . . that would have made Peter proud."

In 1968 he helped launch *60 Minutes*, where he became famous as a pit bull in a nicely tailored suit. "He was fearless and could ask questions that you can't even dream up," says correspondent Lesley Stahl. An example among many: During a 1979 sit-down, Wallace asked Iran's Ayatollah Khomeini if he knew that Egyptian president Anwar Sadat had referred to him as a "lunatic." One of his most controversial choices was to show footage of his subject, Dr. Jack Kevorkian, assisting in suicide. "We were accused of crossing the line," he said. But "we thought it was in the public interest."

Late in his life Wallace, who married four times, disclosed that he had long battled depression and had once even attempted suicide. Still, he felt extraordinarily lucky about his life. "I've gotten to go around the world and talk to virtually anyone I wanted to, ask them whatever question I wanted to ask," he said. "My God, what a job."

ANDY ROONEY

—

A couple of years ago, Morley Safer was walking down the street with his *60 Minutes* colleague Andy Rooney when a fan stopped Rooney and asked for an autograph. "And Andy said, 'No, I get paid to write,'" recalled Safer. "There wasn't a phony bone in his body." *Curmudgeonly* bones, however, he had aplenty: In 33 years as a *60 Minutes* commentator, he turned avuncular acerbity into a journalistic art form, championing Everyman's struggle with the Sisyphian minutiae—from airline fees to e-books—of daily life. Rooney died of complications from surgery two weeks after giving his final broadcast. "It was such a dignified finish for him," said *60 Minutes* producer Jeff Fager. "He's impossible to replace, on television and as a friend."

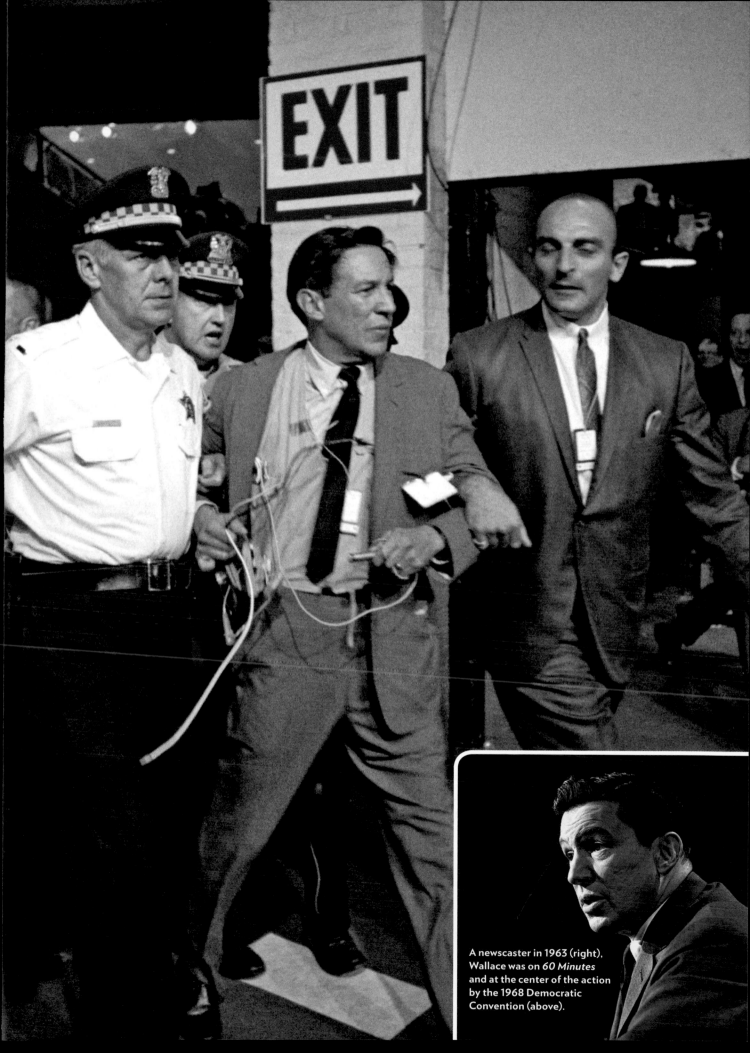

A newscaster in 1963 (right), Wallace was on *60 Minutes* and at the center of the action by the 1968 Democratic Convention (above).

ANDY GRIFFITH

He starred on Broadway in *No Time for Sergeants*, had a second hit TV series with *Matlock* (1986-1995), even won a 1996 Grammy for the gospel album *I Love to Tell the Story: 25 Timeless Hymns*. But for a generation, or two, or three, Andy Griffith will always be *The Andy Griffith Show*'s Sheriff Andy Taylor, widowed father of Opie (Ron Howard) and the wise and genial law in fictional Mayberry, N.C., an idyllic small town populated by vivid comic characters including jittery Deputy Barney Fife (Don Knotts) and mechanic Gomer Pyle (Jim Nabors). "Mayberry was a utopia for a lot of people, like a Norman Rockwell painting," said his friend Dick Van Dyke. Griffith was always careful to say that he wasn't as easygoing as his TV alter-ego—his first two marriages ended in divorce, and he later said he was "not a good father" to his son Sam, who died of a drug overdose in 1996—but such honesty didn't hurt, and perhaps helped, his image. "Andy tapped into an iconic American Everyman hero," said *Matlock* costar Linda Purl. "He gave dignity to the common man."

Sitcom classmates (clockwise from top left): John Travolta, Hegyes, Palillo, Hilton-Jacobs

ROBERT HEGYES
—
RON PALILLO

The year saw the passing of two of prime-time TV's Sweathogs, the nickname for the lovable misfit foursome Gabe Kaplan taught in the hit '70s sitcom *Welcome Back, Kotter* that made classmate John Travolta a star. Both Ron Palillo, 63, who played adenoidal goofball Arnold Horshack, and Robert Hegyes, 60, a.k.a. wiseguy streetkid Juan Luis Pedro Phillipo de Huevos Epstein, succumbed to heart attacks.

SHERMAN HELMSLEY

In the heyday of Norman Lear sitcoms, Sherman Hemsley, as *The Jefferson*'s patriarch, provided memorable counterpoint to *All in the Family*-man Archie Bunker. The latter saw the world through the prism of an aggrieved white workingman, fighting a rearguard action as the times changed faster than he could. Hemsley's George Jefferson, a tetchy entrepreneur who proudly chipped away at the bastions Bunker defended, was just as hypersensitively, comically and, often, wrongly focussed on matters of race—from the opposite perspective. That he made the character a prime-time favorite for a decade is a tribute to the skills that Hemsley (who, in real life, described himself as "just an old hippie—you know, peace and love") brought to the small screen.

ROBIN GIBB

—

There were records before—including the hits "Massachusetts" (1967) and "I Started a Joke" (1968)—and after, but the Bee Gees will always be associated with the *Saturday Night Fever* soundtrack, which launched them almost as high as leader Barry Gibb's trademark falsetto. The hits ("Stayin' Alive," "How Deep Is Your Love," and "You Should Be Dancing"), the hair and the skintight candy-colored leisure suits helped define the disco era, and left all three brothers Gibb—twin Maurice and old brother Barry rounded out the supergroup—free, for the rest of their lives, to pursue any interest they had. Robin, 62, was working on a music project, Titanic Requiem, with his son RJ when he succumbed to colon cancer. In an interview shortly before his death, he offered no complaints. "It's been a magic carpet ride," he said, "with so many magical moments."

ADAM YAUCH

The three-headed Jerry Lewises of rap, the Beastie Boys bottled a cultural moment with 1986's "(You Gotta) Fight for Your Right (to Party)" and, arguably, helped make the world safe for Eminem. But beneath the bluster lurked—good heavens!— some sincerity and seriousness: Cofounder Adam "MCA" Yauch, who once described the Beasties partying persona as "a joke that just went too far," embraced Buddhism and cofounded the Milarepa Fund, which has organized benefit concerts and raised awareness about Tibetan issues. Yauch, 47, died in May after a three-year battle with cancer. Fellow Beastie and lifelong friend Michael "Mike D" Diamond praised Yauch's faith, humor and humility: "The world is in need of many more like him."

DICK CLARK

During his three decades at the helm of *American Bandstand*, Dick Clark showcased hundreds of singers from Buddy Holly to Michael Jackson, introduced America to dance crazes and even helped integrate TV. "He wasn't one to take no for an answer," said Jeff Margolis, Clark's longtime producer. "When he decided to revolutionize the music business, he did it. We all say that we went to the University of Dick Clark."

His famously ageless face and neatly groomed hair spawned a generation of TV hosts—Ryan Seacrest calls him "my inspiration"—and earned him the nickname America's Oldest Teenager. (The secret to eternal youth? Said Clark: "Pick your parents very carefully.") In an age when TV was lily-white, Clark invited African-American performers and dancers on *Bandstand*. "He made history, and I made history because of him," says singer Chubby Checker, whose "Twist" became a craze after he danced on *Bandstand* in 1960.

There was, however, one thing Clark would not do: "People expect me to dance well," he once admitted. "I don't dance. Period."

EARL SCRUGGS

O ver a six-decade career, the banjo and bluegrass pioneer, who cowrote "The Ballad of Jed Clampett" theme song for TV's *The Beverly Hillbillies*, helped modernize country music with his unique style of pickin' using his thumb and two fingers. Country star Ricky Skaggs says Scruggs was always listening not to himself, but to "the next generation."

DON CORNELIUS

W ith guests including James Brown, Aretha Franklin, Smokey Robinson and LL Cool J, *Soul Train* creator and host Don Cornelius was a primal force in bringing R&B, funk and, later, hip-hop to TV. "He was a pioneer, and innovator, and a trailblazer," Earvin "Magic" Johnson, basketball legend and Soul Train Holdings chairman, said in a statement. "He was the first African-American to create, produce, host and, more importantly, own his own television show."

The Warriors: Ali (left) and Frazier in 1993, 18 years after their epic battle in Manilla.

JOE FRAZIER

—

Having learned about self-promotion from the flamboyant wrestler Gorgeous George—make people angry, and they'll pay to watch you get beat—Muhammad Ali took the tactic to the extreme in his three legendary bouts with "Smokin' Joe" Frazier, viciously mocking his opponent as an "Uncle Tom" and a "gorilla." Frazier, who had supported Ali during his fight to avoid the draft during the Vietnam War, was hurt—and incensed. Although Ali apologized, Frazier, unmollified, would later seem to suggest that Ali's long decline after their 1975 Thrilla in Manilla, one of the most brutal heavyweight fights on record, won by Ali, was proof of who really won that fight.

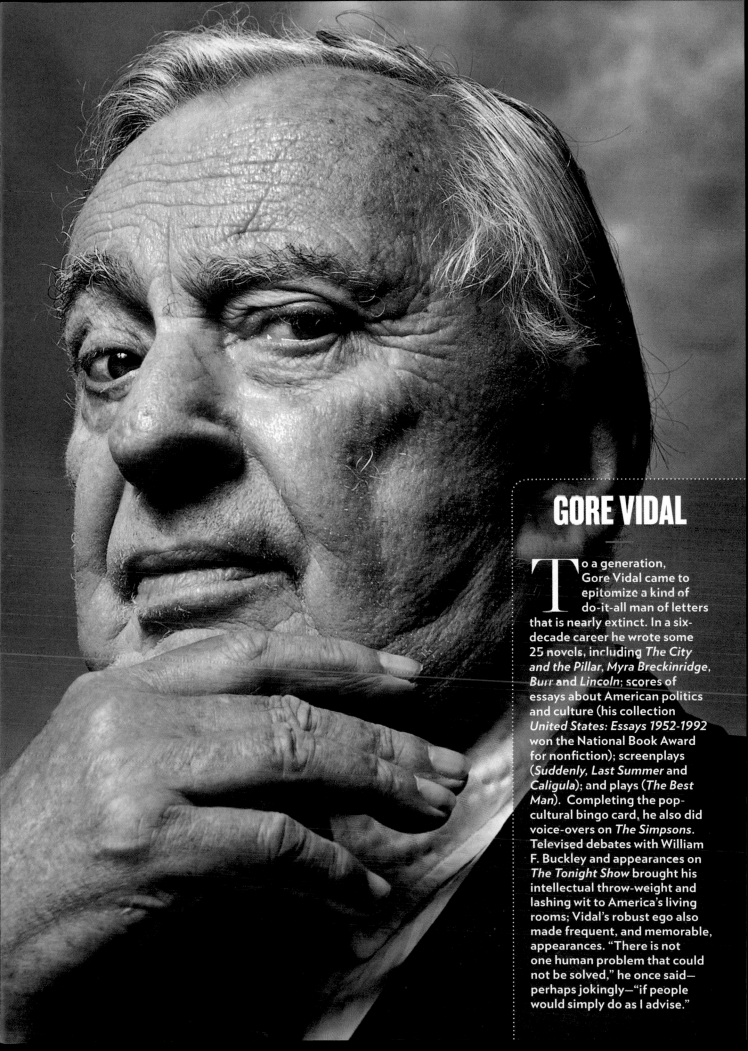

GORE VIDAL

To a generation, Gore Vidal came to epitomize a kind of do-it-all man of letters that is nearly extinct. In a six-decade career he wrote some 25 novels, including *The City and the Pillar*, *Myra Breckinridge*, *Burr* and *Lincoln*; scores of essays about American politics and culture (his collection *United States: Essays 1952-1992* won the National Book Award for nonfiction); screenplays (*Suddenly, Last Summer* and *Caligula*); and plays (*The Best Man*). Completing the pop-cultural bingo card, he also did voice-overs on *The Simpsons*. Televised debates with William F. Buckley and appearances on *The Tonight Show* brought his intellectual throw-weight and lashing wit to America's living rooms; Vidal's robust ego also made frequent, and memorable, appearances. "There is not one human problem that could not be solved," he once said—perhaps jokingly—"if people would simply do as I advise."

RICHARD DAWSON

—

A Brit comic who later starred as safe-cracking Cpl. Newkirk on *Hogan's Heroes* (1965-1971), Dawson found his true calling hosting the game show *Family Feud* in 1976. He had two signatures: the catchphrase "Survey says!" and a penchant for kissing female contestants—an estimated 20,000 during his 10 seasons, one of whom, Gretchen Johnson, became his second wife. The onstage showbiz-ness was mostly an act, said his son Gary, who called his father "an amazing talent, a loving husband, a great dad and doting grandfather." As Dawson himself once told PEOPLE, "I may be smarmy, but I must be doing something right."

ERNEST BORGNINE

Baby Boomers knew him as the commander of PT73 in the classic '60s sitcom *McHale's Navy*, which ran for four seasons. But their older siblings, and parents, knew a different Borgnine, who appeared, often as the heavy, in more than 120 films including 1953's *From Here to Eternity* with Frank Sinatra. But it was the revelation of a softer side, as a sad Bronx butcher in *Marty* (1955), that brought Borgnine his Oscar—against an all-star list of nominees that year which included Sinatra, Spencer Tracy, James Cagney and James Dean.

PHYLLIS DILLER

—

She was a housewife and mother of six when, at 37, she decided to try comedy. It worked, for nearly six decades. "She was a stand-up comic when females did not stand up," said her manager, Milt Suchin. "She was a trail-blazer." Her trademark cackle and sassy self-deprecation made her one-of-a-kind—and didn't disappear offstage. "She had a magnetic cockroach that she'd slide across the table when we were having dinner, and people would scream," says Suchin. "That was her sense of humor." And, yes, she really did loathe domestic chores: "She really was the unhappy house-wife," says pal Joan Rivers. "She didn't like housework. One of her great jokes was 'I love to serve chocolate cake because it doesn't show the dirt.'"

ABOVE: One small step for man: "He was . . . a very quiet individual," said fellow astronaut Jim Lovell. "But when he spoke, people listened."

NEIL ARMSTRONG

Only one person could be the first to walk on the moon, and the choice of Neil Armstrong was no accident. The first "would be a legend, an American hero," Chris Kraft, NASA's director of flight operations, told Armstrong's biographer. "Neil was Neil. Calm, quiet and absolute confidence . . . He had no ego." In the end, Kraft said, "Neil Armstrong, reticent, soft-spoken, and heroic, was our only choice."

His was, indeed, the story of an American hero: Born in Wapakoneta, Ohio, he learned to fly at 15, and later flew 78 combat missions over Korea. After his epic space moment, he shied from publicity, credited others and went on to teach aeronautical engineering at the University of Cincinnati. His reasoning? "We all like to be recognized not for one piece of fireworks but for the ledger of our daily work," he said. His family asked that anyone who wanted to pay tribute to the memory of Armstrong, who died at 82 following heart surgery, "honor his example of service, accomplishment and modesty."

ETTA JAMES

She was only 15 when she had her first hit, "Dance with Me Henry," and toured with Little Richard. That was nearly six decades ago; Etta James—born Jamesetta Hawkins—would go on to win four Grammys while staking out her own territory on the border of jazz and rhythm and blues. Her greatest hits include "Tell Mama" and "Something's Got a Hold on Me"—and the song heard at virtually every wedding since she recorded her classic 1961 rendition, "At Last."

SALLY RIDE

On June 18, 1983, she soared into space and became an overnight sensation. But the first American woman to reach the stars shunned celebrity. "My intention," she told PEOPLE at the time, "is to come back to the astronaut office and get back in line and try and fly again." The perfectly named Ride would complete two missions on the *Challenger*, wittily fielding offensive questions from the media (asked if she'd wear a bra in space, she retorted, "There is no sag in zero-g") and inspiring millions of girls to give their dreams a shot. Ride died, at 61, of pancreatic cancer.

The Band, in 1971 (from left): Garth Hudson, Robbie Robertson, Helm, Richard Manuel, Rick Danko.

LEVON HELM
—

Four of its members were Canadians, but the great rock quintet the Band had a distinctly Southern sound—and much of that came from the iconic voice of drummer Levon Helm, the pride of Turkey Scratch, Ark. Helm's vocal instrument—plaintive, proud, lonesome—defined their classic hits "The Weight," "The Night They Drove Old Dixie Down" and "Up on Cripple Creek." Stricken with throat cancer in the '90s, Helm began gathering musician pals to put on fund-raising concerts in his Woodstock, N.Y., barn; the shows, called Midnight Rambles, eventually drew fans from around the world and helped create two albums, *Dirt Farmer* and *Electric Dirt*, that earned Helm, who died at 71, three late-career Grammys.

MAURICE SENDAK

He wrote and illustrated some of the most beloved children's books of all time—though that was not necessarily his intention. "I don't write for children," Maurice Sendak said. "I write. And somebody says, 'That's for children.' I don't sit down to make children happy. I like them as few and far between as I do adults." Comically curmudgeon, Sendak, who died at 83 of complications following a stroke, loathed the "trite" predictability of most kidlit and infused his stories with complexity; his signature work, *Where the Wild Things Are*, depicts a naughty boy who, after being sent to bed without supper, sails off to a land of equally naughty monsters. "He understood children's toughness, cruelty and vulnerability," said playwright Tony Kushner, a close friend. "He made art out of all of it."

MICHAEL CLARKE DUNCAN

Best known for his Academy Award-nominated portrayal of a death-row inmate with mystical powers in the 1999 drama *The Green Mile*, Duncan, 54, suffered a heart attack in L.A. in July and passed away seven weeks later, according to his fiancée, Omarosa Manigault-Stallworth, 38, former star of *The Apprentice*. "I am terribly saddened at the loss of Big Mike," said his *Green Mile* costar Tom Hanks. "He was the treasure we all discovered on the set of *The Green Mile*. He was magic. He was a big love of man and his passing leaves us stunned." Later, an emotional Hanks, speaking at a memorial service for Duncan, told an anecdote about his friend that got so many laughs it went viral on YouTube, recording more than 1.6 million hits.

When he died at 93 in Dublin, Ga., Karl Slover was one of the last Munchkins from 1939's *The Wizard of Oz*. Born in Czechoslovakia, he stopped growing at age 4, and his father had doctors use a stretching machine to try to make him taller. When that failed, his father sold him to a troupe of traveling midgets from Berlin. The 4' 4" Slover, who played a trumpeter, soldier and townsman in *Oz*, noted that Dorothy's terrier Toto earned more than he did.

KARL SLOVER

LIFE IN OZ: As one of the 124 actors who portrayed Munchkins, Slover recalled the Oz shoot as grueling. "But three years later," he told the *Times* in 2007, "when I saw the movie, I really enjoyed it."

CREDITS

—

Editor Cutler Durkee
Design Director Andrea Dunham
Photo Director Chris Dougherty
Photo Editor C. Tiffany Lee-Ramos
Art Director Cynthia Rhett
Designer Joan Dorney
Writers Steve Dougherty, Kristen Mascia
Writer/Reporter Ellen Shapiro
Copy Editor Will Becker
Scanners Brien Foy, Salvador Lopez, Stephen Pabarue **Group Imaging Director** Francis Fitzgerald
Imaging Manager Rob Roszkowski
Imaging Production Managers Charles Guardino, Romeo Cifelli, Jeffrey Ingledue

Special thanks: Céline Wojtala, David Barbee, Jane Bealer, Patricia Clark, Margery Frohlinger, Suzy Im, Ean Sheehy, Patrick Yang

TIME HOME ENTERTAINMENT
Publisher Jim Childs
Vice President, Business Development & Strategy Steven Sandonato
Executive Director, Marketing Services Carol Pittard **Executive Director, Retail & Special Sales** Tom Mifsud **Executive Publishing Director** Joy Butts **Director, Bookazine Development & Marketing** Laura Adam **Finance Director** Glenn Buonocore **Associate Publishing Director** Megan Pearlman **Assistant General Counsel** Helen Wan **Assistant Director, Special Sales** Ilene Schreider **Book Production Manager** Suzanne Janso **Design & Prepress Manager** Anne-Michelle Gallero **Brand Manager** Michela Wilde **Associate Prepress Manager** Alex Voznesenskiy **Associate Brand Manager** Isata Yansaneh **Editorial Director** Stephen Koepp **Editorial Operations Director** Michael Q. Bullerdick

Special thanks:
Katherine Barnet, Jeremy Biloon, Susan Chodakiewicz, Rose Cirrincione, Lauren Hall Clark, Jacqueline Fitzgerald, Christine Font, Jenna Goldberg, Hillary Hirsch, David Kahn, Amy Mangus, Robert Marasco, Kimberly Marshall, Amy Migliaccio, Nina Mistry, Dave Rozzelle, Ricardo Santiago, Adriana Tierno, Vanessa Wu